Anonymous

**Thoughts on the present East India Bill passed into a Law**

Anonymous

**Thoughts on the present East India Bill passed into a Law**

ISBN/EAN: 9783337059170

Printed in Europe, USA, Canada, Australia, Japan

Cover: Foto ©ninafisch / pixelio.de

More available books at **www.hansebooks.com**

# THOUGHTS

ON THE

PRESENT

EAST INDIA BILL:

PASSED INTO A LAW, AUGUST 1784.

TO WHICH IS ADDED,

## AN AUTHENTIC COPY OF THE BILL.

LONDON:

PRINTED FOR JOHN STOCKDALE,

OPPOSITE

BURLINGTON-HOUSE, PICCADILLY.

MDCCLXXXIV.

PRICE TWO SHILLINGS.

# THOUGHTS, &c.

OF all the topics which have at different periods attracted the attention of a free and enlightened People, there is none which contains matter of more serious enquiry, than that which forms the subject of the following pages. A second plan has now been received in Parliament, for the future government of our possessions in India; and while the principles on which it is founded, and the measures which it adopts, are debated by our Representatives, it well becomes us to look with a careful and jealous eye, to the event of a discussion in which all our dearest interests are involved. And, indeed, great as this question must at any time have appeared, extensive in its objects, and formidable in its consequences, there are many circumstances which concur to render it inte-

resting

resting to us, in the present moment, even much beyond its natural importance.

It is, in the first place, a consideration which deeply involves the credit of our Government, and the honour of our Nation. We are bound by every feeling of humanity, justice, and religion, to provide some remedy for the multiplied oppressions under which the natives of India have groaned. We are bound by our duty to ourselves, as well as to them, no longer to suffer the establishment of the British Nation in that climate, to remain the scourge and curse of its unfortunate inhabitants. That it has hitherto been so, there is too much reason to believe; and allowing in the statements which have been made on that head to the Public, for the extravagance of a heated imagination, and the intemperance of party zeal, much still remains uncontroverted, a reproach to our feelings, and a disgrace to our national character. It is incumbent on us, therefore, to wipe away this stain; and by whatever means we now find ourselves substituted in the place of the natural rulers of that country, we must be guided in our future conduct towards it, by

that

that firſt duty of thoſe who govern, the con-
ſulting the eaſe and happineſs of their ſub-
jects.

Nor is our own political welfare leſs at ſtake.
By a diſgraceful and ruinous war, our burthens
have been more increaſed, and our reſources
more diminiſhed, in the ſhort ſpace of nine
calamitous years, than in a whole preceding
century of proſperity and triumph. Much,
therefore, does it behove us to cheriſh what is
ſtill ours; to guard well the remnants of a
great and flouriſhing empire; and to prove, by
a juſt and prudent adminiſtration of our remaining territories, that we have not drunk,
without benefit, of the bitter cup of adverſity
and humiliation.

To theſe circumſtances, which mark the ne-
ceſſity and magnitude of the object, is to be
added, the difficulty of the means by which it
is to be attained. We are to weigh the diſtance
of the country to be governed, the inveteracy
of the abuſes to be reformed, the power of
delinquents, the hopes of impunity, and the
temptations to guilt: Conſiderations now certainly

tainly pointed, and brought home to our feelings, by the extent and tendency of that plan, which was attempted on thefe grounds to be defended. But great indeed muft have been their weight, and infinite their importance, if they could have reconciled this country to the admiffion of the fmalleft part of thofe principles, which were thus to have been eftablifhed. Even as a Commercial People, we fhould, undoubtedly, have feen with horror, the annihilation of our firft Trading Company; but as a Nation jealous of our Freedom, we looked from that meafure to confequences of far greater importance. We faw that it was intended to deftroy, at one blow, every legal fecurity under which our property was enjoyed: That it was meant in the fame moment to eftablifh in the hands of a powerful Faction, an Executive Government, independent of the Crown : That to this Government was to be given the abfolute and uncontrouled dominion of the Eaft, including in it patronage, influence, and power, far beyond what is vefted in our own Sovereign; and ftill further, that to thefe perfons, thus exalted above the level, not of their fellow-fubjects only, but of their King,

and

and of the Government of their Country, there
was to be given a PERMANENCY of Power, unknown to any part of our Conftitution, and
abfolutely incompatible with the very nature of
a Free State. Seeing all this, we felt a neceffity greater than any which was urged to us;
and we declared, with one voice, that it was
defirable that former abufes fhould be corrected;
that it was to be wifhed, that India might be
well governed ; *but that it was* NECESSARY *that
the* PEOPLE OF GREAT BRITAIN *fhould continue*
FREE.

In a happy hour for this kingdom, that plan
mifcarried, which, if it had fucceeded, would
have given an abfolute power, under the cloak
of reformation, to perfons undiftinguifhed in
their country, except by a blind attachment
to one daring and ambitious Leader. And we
have now the fatisfaction to fee, that there are
among us men of no mean abilities, of no tri-
fling knowledge in public bufinefs, and above
all, of no inconfiderable experience in this particular branch of it; who, while they acknow-
ledge the importance, extent, and difficulty of
the evil, are confident of removing it, by an
operation

operation lefs violent in its execution, and lefs
alarming in its effects. A plan has now been
propofed, and has received the marked approbation of Parliament, which profeffes to relieve
public credit without *annihilating* \* the firft
Trading Company in the world; to fecure to
us the enjoyment of our territories without endangering our conftitution; and to protect the
natives of India, without enflaving the people of
Great Britain.

And yet, much as we muft all defire the accomplifhment of thefe hopes, let us not be deceived

---

\* In the debate on the Commitment of the prefent
India bill, Mr. F-x was pleafed to fay, that he had never
denied that *his* plan would have gone to the *total annihilation*
of the Eaft India Company. The Writer of thefe pages
affirms, that Mr. F-x has repeatedly made that denial, as
may be feen by a reference to any of the printed debates
of the laft Seffion. And it is, left this admiffion fhould
again be retracted, that it is thought proper *here* to record
it. Among all the arts ufed to deceive the people into an
approbation of meafures which they abhor, there is none
lefs juftifiable than the conftant mifreprefentation of Parliamentary debates in almoft every public paper, which it
known to be the daily employment of more than one of
Mr. F-x's moft active friends.

- ceived by them into an indiscriminate approbation of the measure on which they are founded.
Let us weigh maturely the objections which are
raised against it ; and having compared it not
only with the former plan (which all condemn)
but with the nature of the object proposed, and
with the means by which that object can be ob-
tained, let us try it on the grounds of reason,
and on the principles of the Constitution. We
may then form an impartial and decided judgement, to which we shall adhere, returning with
contempt the daily insults of those who treat
our opinions as the effects of popular delusion
and temporary frenzy. Those very men know,
and have reason to lament, that the people of
Great Britain are not so weak as *they* were wil-
ling to believe. They have found in us judgement to discern, and firmness to resist, their
plans for our oppression. They will ever find it
so : And till they have persuaded us to surren-
der up our reason, they will in vain attempt to
undermine our liberties ; nor will they DARE to
seize them, till they have acquired the power
to crush us.

C                                        It

It is therefore to my fellow-citizens, to an uninfluenced and difcerning Public, to men capable of judging what is right, and defirous of following it, that I wifh to fubmit my ideas on this fubject; and I will proceed without further preface, to the confideration of the plan now propofed, which naturally divides itfelf into three diftinct objects.

Firft, The eftablifhing a Power of Controul in this kingdom, by which the Executive Government in India is to be connected with that over the reft of the Empire.

Secondly, The regulating the Conduct of the Company's Servants in India, in order to remedy the evils which have prevailed there.

Thirdly, The providing for the punifhment of thofe perfons who fhall, neverthelefs, continue in the practice of crimes which have brought difgrace upon their country.

To each of thefe, various objections have been raifed, which it is my intention to confider feparately; and with them, the fpirit and tendency of the regulations to which they apply.

---

I. The neceffity of connecting, in fome meafure, the Executive Government of India with that of this country, has long been univerfally felt, was adopted in the former plan, is acknowledged by the oppofers of this, and has in the form now propofed received the confent of the Company. But it is a very material point to confider, how this may be fufficiently accomplifhed, keeping at the fame time in view the rights of the Company, and having an attentive and watchful eye to the Conftitution of this country.

With refpect to the rights of the Company, it is perhaps enough for us to confider, that they have themfelves pointed out this mode as confiftent with their ideas, and agreeable to their wifhes. If any thing more were wanted on this head, the very nature of the objection which has been made to it in Parliament, fufficiently entitles it to our approbation. The fupporters of the former Bill, (and in this inftance

they

they certainly act confiftently with their paft conduct, however inconfiftently with the laws of juftice, and the principles of the Conftitution) complain that TOO LITTLE is now to be wrefted from the Company. That *too little* fhould be refumed by Parliament, of that which has been granted by Charter; that a Minifter fhould take into his own hands *too little* power, *too little* influence, and *too little* patronage, is a complaint which might well weigh with thofe who fupported government, only* in confidence that they would diftribute corruptly what they had feized violently; and that they would fhare the plunder among thofe who had affifted in the robbery. But in the eyes of a virtuous and confiderate people, it would, if it were neceffary, overbalance many objections, and compenfate for many faults.

It is, however, by no means fufficient to avoid trenching on the rights of the Company, unlefs the plan to be adopted holds out a reafonable hope of regulation in India, without creating

* I am far from including in this defcription all who voted for Mr. Fox's Bill: Many certainly did fo confcientioufly, being deceived into it by fpecious, though inconclufive arguments.

creating in any perſon whatever a degree of
power formidable to the Conſtitution of theſe
kingdoms. On both theſe heads objections have
been raiſed; and Mr. *Fox* has aſſured us, that
the Power of Controul now to be created, is ina-
dequate to any purpoſe of Reform, while an
alarming acceſſion of Influence is at the ſame time
to be given by it to the Crown. Let us, therefore, recur to the Bill itſelf, in order to examine
theſe aſſertions, and to decide whether they are
juſtified by any ſolid ground of argument, or
are the ſuggeſtions of a gloomy and diſappointed
mind, brooding over the loſs both of popularity
and power, and lamenting too late the conſe-
quence of an impatient thirſt for abſolute dominion, an intemperate and " *vaulting ambition*,
" *which o'erleapt itſelf—and fell on th' other ſide!*"

In the firſt place, therefore, with regard to
the regulation of India, we ſhall find on exa-
mination, that this Bill, while it leaves to the
Company the entire management of their commercial concerns; while it continues in the
Directors choſen by the Company, the conduct
of their political affairs, provides, nevertheleſs,
that they ſhall not be permitted to depart from
thoſe

thofe maxims of government there, on which all men are agreed. And if they fhould be inclined to forfake the principles of œconomy, peace, and juftice, it prevents their endangering by fuch conduct, both the interefts of the Company and the profperity of the Empire at large. In thefe inftances they will be controuled by perfons connected with the Executive Government for the time being, appointed under his Majefty's Commiffion, and daily refponfible to Parliament for every circumftance in the execution of their office. Thus it is, that by the eftablifhment of that in which the genius of our Conftitution delights, a fpecies of mixed government, every advantage is held out, which can arife from mutual emulation for the public good, from local knowledge, from experience in the detail of bufinefs, from perfonal intereft in the well-being of the Company, added to a permanent fyftem of policy, to the exertion of political talents, and the refponfibility of executive office.

Still, however, with all thefe circumftances, and with the addition of every method which prudence can fuggeft, to enforce from the

servants

fervants abroad a ftrict obdience to the orders
which they receive from hence, this government has been ftigmatized as weak and ineffi-
cient. And it is certainly true, that it poffeffes
neither the unlimited PATRONAGE, nor the
unconftitutional PERMANENCY, which Mr.
Fox had provided for *his* Commiffioners. To
the feven perfons of his nomination he had
given (in the words of a fpirited and unanfwer-
able publication *) " the whole influence of
" the offices of every kind, in India and at
" home, belonging to the Company ; and the
" whole influence arifing from the tranfactions
" of their trade, in the purchafe of goods for
" exportation, furnifhing fhipping, ftores, and
" recruits ; the influence arifing from the
" method of felling their goods, by bringing
" forward or keeping back goods at the fales,
" or giving indulgencies as to payments, fo as
" to accommodate thofe who were meant to
" be favoured ; the influence arifing from the
" favour they might fhew to thofe who were
" then in England, and had left debts or ef-
                                        " fects

* Mr. Pulteney's Pamphlet on Mr. Fox's Eaft India
Bill; printed for J. Stockdale, Piccadilly.

" fects in India, as to the mode of bringing
" home and recovering their fortunes; the
" influence of contracts of all kinds in India;
" of promotions from step to step; of favour
" in the inland trade; of intimidation with re-
" spect to every perfon then there, who might
" come home with a fortune, both with regard
" to recovering his debts, and the means of re-
" mittance, and with regard to enquiries into
" his conduct; the influence upon Foreign
" Companies or Foreign States, who have
" eftablifhments in that country, who, in re-
" turn, might have the means of acting upon
" individuals in this country; the influence
" upon the native Princes of India; fome of
" whom have already found the way of pro-
" curing the Elections of Members of Parlia-
" ment; and many other means of influence,
" which it is impoffible to forefee or to trace :"
All this he had given, *if his affertions are to
be believed*, not to ftrengthen any Faction, or
eftablifh any Ariftocracy in this country; but
with the fole view of providing a ftrong Government in India.

Thofe

Thofe who have framed the prefent plan appear to have reafoned differently. They feem not to have imagined, that Subordination, the firft principle of ftrong Government, can be promoted by teaching inferior fervants to look from their fuperiors to an intereft at home, both for advancement and protection; or, that we can expect among them any emulation for the public fervice, if we veft here the power of reward, in perfons who can have neither leifure nor opportunity to know their merit, or to enquire into their pretenfions. Perhaps, alfo, they carried their reafoning further, and concluded that the Princes of India would not the more refpect our Governors for being neglected by thofe whom they were fent to command: While the fuperior fervants themfelves would not with much chearfulnefs intruft to perfons, having no dependence on them, and in whom they repofed no confidence, meafures of much delicacy in their execution, and involving in their confequences the deareft interefts of the Company and the Public.

D                    But

But it is alſo true, that this Board is not
*permanent.* That, if the Adminiſtration of
this country be changed, they muſt alſo ſhare
its fate, and make way for perſons connected
with thoſe to whoſe care his Majeſty ſhall
intruſt the reſt of his dominions. If it were
not ſo, What would be our ſituation ? The
general intereſts of the Empire would be directed by men of one deſcription, while India
would be under the command of others in
oppoſition to the King's Government, perhaps
on points intimately connected with Indian
politics. Is it ſufficient to ſay, that in this
caſe the latter would be *removed* by an addreſs
of Parliament ? If ſo, Where is this boaſted
*permanency ?* If whenever a difference of
opinion aroſe, the Indian Board was to be removed, that it might not continue at variance
with the Cabinet, then is this ſyſtem aban-
doned as impracticable, in the only moment
in which it could be uſeful : And the whole
plainly appears to have been what we have
unanimouſly declared it, a plan not for a permanency of meaſures, but a permanency of
MEN ; a permanency of patronage, influence,
and

and power, to an Ariftocracy already formidable to the liberties of their country.

The laft objection which is made to this
part of the Bill, can fcarcely be thought to
merit a ferious confideration. Mr. Fox having
made a general charge ·againft the prefent
Adminiftration, of defiring to increafe the
Influence of the Crown, thought it neceffary,
in confidering this capital feature of their
Government, to affert that it bore that com-
plexion. But he *afferted* it only : He did
attempt, for he knew that he was not able, to
prove it : The undeniable fact being, that
the Bill gives to the Crown *no influence whatever*, civil or military, at home or abroad ;
vefting only in the King, as the legitimate
Executive Power of this Empire, the appointment of perfons to controul the Executive
Government of India, *without falaries, and
without patronage.*

Thus then, on a view of the provifions held
out by this plan, for conftituting at home a
Superintending Government for the dominions
of this country in the Eaft, it appears, that

the

the end propofed to us, will be accomplifhed without the mifchiefs which were thought to accompany it. With the full confent of the Company, and confequently without any violation of property or charters, we fhall eftablifh a power fufficient effectually to reform the abufes, and controul the Government of India, without having given either to individuals, or to the Crown, any authority dangerous to our own liberties.

---

II. Nor is this Board left at large, like the defpotic Commiffion of Mr. *Fox*, to exercife their fuperintending power, as caprice or inexperience may dictate. Regulations are provided, and a fyftem of policy marked out for them, under which alone our dominions in India can be made productive of advantage or honour to this country. And thefe relate to the fecond head under which I propofed to confider this Bill; as eftablifhing rules for the conduct of the Company's fervants in India, in order to remedy the evils that have prevailed in that quarter.

Of

Of thefe evils, the firft and moft ftriking
feems to be, the unfettled ftate of the Government, exhibiting a ftruggle of clafhing powers,
with little order or fubordination. It has been
our miftaken policy, to controul the power of
the feveral Governors, by the addition of four
Affiftant Counfellors, any three of whom com-
bined, may thwart the meafures which the Governor brings forward, fo as entirely to fuper-
fede his authority, To the difunion and dif-
traction of Boards thus conftituted, we may
refer the bulk of thofe misfortunes which we
are now lamenting, and againft which we wifh
to provide in future : Not entering into the
queftions in iffue between the feveral Parties,
but juftly concluding, that the permanent adop-
tion of almoft any fyftem would have been at-
tended with lefs evil, than a fcene of conten-
tion, which degraded the dignity, and of fluc-
tuation, which deftroyed the energy, of the
Britifh Government. Wifely, therefore, have
the Framers of this Bill begun with reftoring
order at the helm ; for which purpofe they
have reduced the number of Counfellors to
three, and given the cafting vote, in cafes of
equality, to the Governor : Thus fecuring to
him

him an efficient fupport to his Adminiftration, except in thofe cafes only where his conduct fhall be difapproved by all thofe who are joined in commiffion with him.

And here let us carefully guard againft the common error of confidering this, and other meafures, with a view to the characters of particular individuals. Such confiderations are ill adapted to the decifion of great and important queftions of policy; becaufe, with them we are too apt to mix our perfonal affections, paffions, and refentments.—If the Bill propofed by Mr. *Fox* did eftablifh in this country a new Government, fuperior to our Laws, and dangerous to our Conftitution, it was a poor argument, to reft its defence on the *characters* of the *individuals* in whom that Government was to be created. Had thofe characters been fuch as they were reprefented; had they been all, *as they certainly were not*, men of acknowledged and tried abilities, with minds unbiaffed by party, and untainted by diffipation and extravagance, that would have been a fmall confolation to us for the furrender of our liberties. In the fame manner, in confidering the power

to

to be given by the present plan to the Governor General of Bengal *for the time being*, let us
be biassed neither by the panegyrists of Mr.
Hastings to approve, nor by his calumniators
to condemn it. Its propriety is grounded on
general principles of government. If he has
abused his former power, let him be recalled
from his situation; if he has used it to the
advantage of the Company, and the Country,
let him be continued in it; but at all events,
let that person, whoever he may be, to whom
we entrust the government, be invested with
weight, power, and efficiency to support it.

Another evil under which we have laboured,
is the want of a Systematic Government, unit-
ing all the British Dependencies in India in the
pursuit of the same objects, and in the obser-
vance of the same plans of policy. We have
seen our Empire there distracted by the different views of distinct Governments, negociating
in opposition to each other; and by their divi-
sions, weakening the power, and disgracing the
character of the British Nation. This is removed by the establishment of a *supreme power*
on that Continent, to which all the other Governments

vernments are made *fubordinate*. By this Bill
there is given to the Governor and Council of
*Bengal* a Controul over the other Prefidencies,
in all points which relate to any tranfactions
with the Country Powers, to peace or war, or
to the application of their forces or revenues:
It is by this fyftem alone that we can infure, in
the exercife of Executive Power, either ftrength
and efficacy abroad, or obedience and refponfibility at home. It conduces to the increafe
of our authority, and the prefervation of our
public faith in India, to teach the natives to
have recourfe, in their tranfactions with us, to
one center of Government; whilft it is effential
to the efficacy of a controul in England, that
there fhould be *one* body to receive orders, and
to anfwer to this country for their execution.

For it muft not be forgotten, that while we
eftablifh the dependency of the inferior Pref-
dencies upon the Council of Bengal abroad,
they are equally fubjected to the direction of
the Company at home. To them there is left
no power of declaring war, of commencing
hoftilities, or forming treaties at pleafure. In
all cafes, except thofe of immediate danger,

and

and absolute neceffity, they are reftrained from
acting without orders received from hence.
This feems to be the moft effectual method of
fecuring to us that pacific fyftem which the
Bill holds out, as confonant to the wifh, the
honour, and the policy of the Britifh Nation.

The next object that comes under the provifions of this Bill, is the redrefs of the grie-
vances of the Natives of India : An object of
which all men muft wifh the accomplifhment,
except thofe who have already profited by our
paft negligence, or thofe who looked from it
to future advantages. But in the attainment
of this we muft proceed cautioufly and tempe-
rately; not with prejudice or paffion, not with
the blind zeal of indifcriminate reformers, who
either believe themfelves, or wifh to be believed, virtuous and humane, in proportion
as they are inconfiderate and violent; but with
the equity of impartial judges, and the prudence of wife legiflators. To provide for the
payment of the debts of the Nabob of Arcot,
which are a burthen on his country, difcrimi-
nating at the fame time thofe which have been
juftly incurred, from thofe which have been

E forced

forced upon him by the injuftice and extortion
of Englifh oppreffors : To afcertain the inde-
terminate rights and pretenfions on which fo
many differences have arifen between him and
the Rajah of Tanjore, fomented by Europeans,
for the fupport of their own interefted views :
And laftly, to deliver the Zemindars, and other
native landholders of India, from oppreffion ;
and to fecure to them their poffeffions, by permanent rules of moderation and juftice : Thefe
are points upon which all men are agreed ; and
upon which this Bill enacts fuch regulations as
are well calculated to infure their attainment,
without giving authenticity to unexamined
claims, or attempting in Parliament to fettle
at once the detail of rights, which differ fo
materially, and in fo many effential circumftances.

But it was neceffary to guard not only againft
injuftice, but alfo againft profufion and extravagance, in the adminiftration of the affairs of
a diftant government under a Commercial Company. A material part, therefore, of this
Bill, is directed againft the abufes faid to have
prevailed in the civil and military departments,
enjoining

enjoining a thorough revifal of their eftablifhments; together with a fuppreffion of fuch
places as are found to be ufelefs, and of fuch
expences as may be conveniently avoided. And
in order to prevent any delufive fhew of re-
trenchment in the prefent moment, or any
deviation from the wife fyftem of œconomy at
a future period, this Reform is directed to be
conftantly fubmitted in its whole ftate and pro-
grefs, to the eye of Parliament.

Cadets and Writers have hitherto been fent
to India in fuch unlimited numbers, as to remain a burthen upon the eftablifhments of the
Company; and their appointment was a prin-
cipal means of influence in this country, exer-
cifed either by the Directors, or through them
by former Minifters. No more of thefe are
now to be fent out, till their number is reduced
within the proper complement, which is not
to be exceeded in future.

The recommendations alfo of the Directors
(frequently made at the defire of Minifters)
under which thofe fervants of the Company
who had an intereft in this country, rofe rapidly

and

and by partiality, to the prejudice of induftri-
ous and meritorious men, are now rendered
ineffectual ; and a fyftem is eftablifhed, of fucceffion by feniority : Leaving, however, to
the Councils abroad, that power which is indifpenfable to all Executive Government, of
bringing forward (not by caprice, but by rea-
fons by them to be affigned) any perfons of ex-
traordinary merit or capacity, to thofe fituations
in which they may effectually ferve their country.
Out of this regulation neceffarily flows a limi-
tation of the age of perfons entering upon the
line of Eaft India fervice. For, if no provifion
was made to prevent children in their cradle
being enrolled on the Eftablifhment, they might
be brought by fucceffion to many important
employments, before they arrived at manhood :
Or, on the other hand, perfons advanced in
years might (as has lately been feen in feveral
inftances) be appointed to the ftations of young
men, for the fole purpofe of repairing diffi-
pated fortunes ; and that without the profpect
of being able to do it in the courfe of years,
by regular advancement and legal profit. On
the fame ground, and on that of preventing,
as far as poffible, the mifchief of tainting the
Govern-

Government of that Continent, by introducing
into it the Parties of Great Britain, all perfons
who have refided five years in Europe fince
their return from India, are precluded from
any future re-appointment to offices in that
country ; with the exception, however, which
juftice requires for a certain time, to fuch
perfons as are now here, or have left India
without the knowledge of this provifion.

The laft body of regulations for the Company's fervants in India, apply to Offences
committed in that Country. Regulations of
the kind here brought forward, have been fo
long called for, and fo indifpenfable to the
very exiftence of that Government, that it
would be difficult to imagine an objection
againft them. Security has been derived to
Indian Delinquents, from the circumftance of
their offences being committed within the territories of Indian Princes, fo as not to come
within the cognizance of the Britifh Government. This Act provides againft further eva-
fions of this mifchievous nature, by declaring
the offence equally punifhable, in whatever ter-
ritory of India it is committed. Under the

fpecious name of Prefents, the groffeft extortion has frequently been cloaked; and all attempts to draw a line having proved nugatory, nothing remained but to put an entire ftop to the practice. The Act, therefore, of receiving Prefents, is declared to be in itfelf Extortion, and punifhable by law accordingly. Of the fame kind with thefe are the regulations againft Difobedience of Orders; for grofs inftances of which we need not go very far back into their Hiftory: And alfo againft the bargaining for Offices; a mifchievous practice in all countries, but moft fo in that, where the means of plunder are great; and confequently, the more difhoneft the men, the higher the prices which they can afford to offer, from the profpect of reimburfing themfelves by proportionate peculation. Both of thefe offences are accordingly pronounced Mifdemeanors at Law: And provifion is made, that the guilty perfons fhall not compound for them with the Company, nor ever be reftored to appointments in their fervice.——Two reftrictions more remain, to complete this general head of Regulations in India: One of them binds Collectors and Receivers by oath, from accepting any private gratuity,

gratuity, over and above the legal tribute;
and the other guards againſt Illicit Correſpon-
dence with the Enemies of the Company, and
of Great Britain: Points of general policy
and utility, which I have thought proper to
mention in their place; but upon which men
are too univerſally agreed, to require any
comment or diſcuſſion.

We have ſeen, then, in what ſpirit theſe regulations are dictated; we have judged how
wiſely they are calculated to meet the evils,
and to reform the abuſes, which have exiſted.
May they be proſperous in their effects! May
the intentions of a patriot Miniſter, may the
wiſhes of a virtuous People, in the cauſe of
humanity and juſtice, be crowned with that
ſucceſs which they both ſo amply merit!
We may then ſee the Government of India,
which has hitherto been a medley of diſcor-
dant powers, where nothing was ſupreme,
nothing ſubordinate, exhibiting the picture of
an orderly and ſyſtematic Empire, where every
part has its proper function, and contributes
to the general benefit and harmony of the
whole. We may ſee that ſpot, which has been
for

for fo many years a theatre where avarice and ambition have contended in rapine and violence, henceforward the feat of liberty, humanity, and juftice. The rights of Nature may then be eftablifhed on the ruins of Oppreffion; and the Britifh Government, long the bane of that Continent, may at length become, what we are bound to make it, a Bleffing to India.

III. We come now to confider the remaining part of the Bill, relating to the *Trial of Offences* which have been committed in India. And here, in the firft place, we have that which forms indeed the ground-work of the whole plan, the univerfal confent of all parties, as to the neceffity of the object. For we are told from every fide, that the temptations to guilt in India are fuch as can never be counteracted, but by the utmoft vigour of efficient laws, to be executed not only in that country, but here alfo, at a diftance from local prejudice, from perfonal partiality, from the hopes of favour, and from the dread of power. How much our

our fyftem of Indian Government is in that
refpe&t deficient, may be learned from the en-
couragement which is now held out to delinquents, by recent and ftriking examples of impunity. We have all feen, that perfons accufed of the moft flagrant crimes that can even
in that country be committed, have defeated
every attempt to bring them to punifhment;
and have baffled not only the authority of the
King's Bench, our higheft court of criminal
juftice, but even the majefty and terrors of
Parliament itfelf. And, undoubtedly, it was
not to any remiffnefs in their profecutors, but
to the genius of our courts of law, and to the
very frame and conftitution of a deliberative
affembly, that the perfons here alluded to,
were indebted on thofe occafions. What then
remained, but the ere&tion of fome new Tribunal, to which might be given a power over
thofe offences, which, in the ordinary courfes
of common law, and parliamentary proceeding,
have defied the arm of juftice.

This was ftated by Mr. Fox, when he opened
his Bill to the late Houfe of Commons, as a
point of indifpenfable neceffity, without which

*no* plan for governing India *could* be efficacious.
He poftponed it, however, till the paffing of
his Bill; that is, till by *annihilating the Company*, he fhould have acquired a power which
would have left the Parliament little room for
deliberation on this or any other fubject. The
prefent Minifter has acted differently : He has
prefented to us, at one view, his whole fyftem;
and has fuffered nothing to deter him from
propofing to Parliament all which he judged
neceffary for his object, and confiftent, at the
fame time, with the rights of the Company
and with the Britifh Conftitution. In this, as
in the other difficult but neceffary meafures of
this Seffions, he has proceeded with opennefs
and candour; fhewing that he has no referves
with his country, to whom he is fo largely indebted.

Let us therefore now confider the principles,
on which a plan of Judicature for India fhould
be regulated, as applicable to the end propofed ; and let us examine how far what is
now brought forward, is confonant to thofe
principles, and calculated to produce that end.
Above all other confiderations, in the trial of

Britifh

Britifh Subjects, it is neceſſary to obſerve the cloſeſt adherence to the SPIRIT of the Britiſh Law: Not from any national or local prejudice, but becauſe that ſpirit is the ſpirit of equity, applying equally to every age and every climate, and depending on the immutable principles of univerſal juſtice. And the very ſame reaſon ſhould induce us, on the other hand, to reject all thoſe *forms*, which are purely of a local nature; which being adopted by our anceſtors, in conformity to our own inſtitutions, and with a view to the adminiſtration of one kingdom, are repugnant to the manners of a diſtant people, and are inapplicable to the government of a widely extended empire.

We all know, and the experience of every neighbouring country will convince us, that it is not by forms alone, but by the ſpirit of mild laws, and by the genius of a free government, that Liberty ſubſiſts. In almoſt every monarchy of Europe, the forms of thoſe deliberative aſſemblies are ſtill preſerved, under which their anceſtors enjoyed the bleſſings of Liberty. But it is in the Parliament of Eng-

F 2

land alone that their fpirit is maintained, of force and energy to protect us equally againft the encroachments of arbitrary Monarchy, and againft the defperate attacks of turbulent and daring Factions.

In the formation, therefore, of this Tribunal, it was the duty of the Minifter to look to that which we fo juftly efteem and venerate, the right of *Trial by Jury*. He was to confider what were the real principles which have rendered this inftitution the palladium of our Liberties ; and diftinguifhing thefe from the minute forms, which cannot be applied to Indian Caufes, both from the length, and the nature of the difcuffions they involve, preferve in his new compofition, the effence and fpirit of that to which we owe the freedom of our Conftitution.

And here we need not reft on argument only. The principles of our Conftitution, particularly with relation to this fubject, have been laid down by men of acknowledged character and ability, lawyers, ftatefmen, and philofophers.
The

The names of Hale,* Blackſtone,† and De Lolme,‡ carry with them an authority far ſupe- rior to any which can be derived from the rea- ſonings of theſe pages. To theſe I will refer my Reader, and he will certainly think it a mat- ter of no ſmall weight, when he finds ſuch men agreed on this ſubject, and pointing out unani- mouſly the following principles as the chief ſource of thoſe benefits which they all ſo much commend :—*Firſt*, that the Judicial Power ſhould be placed in hands entirely diſtinct from thoſe in which the Executive Government is lodged :—*Secondly*, that it ſhould be exerciſed by a fluctuating, and not by a permanent body : —And laſtly, that ſuch body ſhould be free from all ſuſpicion of partiality, both by the deſcription of men out of whom it is ſelected, and by the manner in which that ſelection is made.

Let us now examine what are the regulations provided by this Bill, in the eſtabliſhment of a new Tribunal, with a view to conſider how far

they

---

* Vide Hiſt. C. L. c. 12.
† Vide Commentaries, B. III. c. 23.
‡ Vide B. I. c. 9 and 10.

they are confonant to the principles here laid down. And to begin with the means by which a perfon may be brought to trial : Informations might, before this Act, have been filed for the crimes to which they relate, either by the King's Attorney General, in virtue of his office, or by any other perfon, with permiffion from the Court of King's Bench. This right remains precifely the fame, with this addition only, that the Attorney of the Company (who ftand, with refpect to offences committed in India, in the fituation of the Government) has alfo the fame official power, which is given in other cafes only to the Attorney General of the Crown.

The material points, therefore, to be con-fidered, are the conftitution of the Tribunal be-fore whom thefe informations are to be tried, and the mode of proceeding in the decifion of fuch caufes. And if we find thefe fo ordered as to fecure to us the benefits above-mentioned, we fhall conclude that this mode of trial is no real infringement of that which we efteem our birth-right, the Trial by Jury.—That the firft of thefe benefits will be preferved in this Court,

" of

" of being wholly *diſtinct* from the executive
" power" is evident, ſince no one of the perſons
of whom the Court will confiſt, is to be appointed by the Crown, or even admitted to it,
while he exerciſes any office under the Government of the Country.—The Court will alſo
have the ſecond advantage, " in being of a *fluctuating* nature ;" for it will not be one and the
ſame body, conſtituted for the trial of all ſuch
cauſes, but a Tribunal ſelected for the particular
occaſion.—And as to the third advantage, " of
*impartiality*," that is amply ſecured, as well by
the deſcription of men from whom this ſelection is to be made, as by the manner of making it; points which require to be confidered
more particularly.


The pannel or body from whom the Court is
to be ſelected, confiſts of a certain number of
the Members of both Houſes of Parliament,
not choſen indiſcriminately, nor yet by the
nomination of the Majority of either Houſe,
who might be ſuppoſed to be attached to the
Miniſter of the day; but by a mode, by which
due weight is given to all parties and deſcrip-
tions of men. Every Member is to deliver in

a liſt

a lift of forty perfons, whom he moft approves; and thofe whofe names appear on twenty lifts, provided they hold no place under Government, and are not particularly connected with the Company, are to compofe a Lift, to be tranfmitted to the Clerk of the Crown, as proper perfons to ferve on this Tribunal.

Here then we have in effect *a pannel of jury-men*, anfwering to the character of Jurymen in every effential particular; firft, as being diftinct from the magiftracy; next, as being a fluctuating body; and laftly, chofen in fuch a manner as to obviate all partiality. The fimilarity continues in the remaining part of the procefs. The perfon accufed has the fame power as in our criminal law, of making peremptory challenges, and that to the number of thirteen of the Peers, and twenty of the Commons; while the profecutor may make challenges upon fpecial caufe fhewn to the Court. From the number then remaining, four Peers and fix Commoners are drawn by lot: To thefe are joined three of the twelve Judges, to be named by their colleagues, one from each of the Courts. And of thefe thirteen thus felected,

confifts the Tribunal, competent to take cognizance of offences committed in India.

Thus it is, that in the conftitution of this
Court we trace every principle which has been
judged effentially charactcriftic of a Jury. If
the minute forms have not been equally preferved, it is becaufe they have been found neither applicable to the fubject, nor compatible
with the nature of the caufes in queftion ; and
would, if adopted here, fail of all the advantages to which they were directed in the
original inftitution.

It is true that the Jurors here are chofen from
a very different clafs of men. Yet when we
confider what are the objects pointed at in the
choice of Juries, namely, that they fhall be men
of fufficient fubftance to fecure refponfibility,
and enabled by their local knowledge, and ha-
bits of life, to judge of the fact, we fhall per-
ceive that the objects aimed at would be entirely loft, by fubmitting the decifion upon Eaft
Indian offences to thofe men of whom Juries
ordinarily confift. Even in the common practice
of the Britifh Courts, we fee that cafes arife of

too delicate or complicated a nature to be trufted to a common Jury; on which occafions it is ufual for a *fpecial* Jury to be fummoned. The inftances of Indian Trials may well be thought to require fomething ftill *more fpecial*, fomething compofed of perfons of a more enlarged fphere of life, and accuftomed to turn their thoughts to points of national concern. In the room therefore of the common, or fpecial Jurymen, are fubftituted perfons, of minds enlarged by education, improved by habit, and verfed in the detail of political concerns : Selected by the choice of all parties in Parliament from that body, to whom the legiflation of the Empire at large has been committed by their fellow citizens. When we add to the impartiality with which this Pannel is felected, the fimilarity that takes place in the mode of ftriking them off, we fhall fee the advantages of our favourite mode of Trial preferved fo minutely in the conftitution of this Tribunal, that we fhall have every reafon to confide in the juftice of its proceedings. Before fuch a Tribunal as this, the guilty may indeed tremble, but the innocent may approach without fear or apprehenfion.

In

In the manner of their proceeding, greater
alterations have been adopted. For neither
is this Tribunal denied the power of ad-
journing, nor is it reftricted to unanimity
in its verdict; it unites alfo the double capacity of Judge and Jury, by deciding not
only upon the Fact, but the Law, and proceeding even to the laft particular of pro-
nouncing fentence.

As to the power of adjournment, it is eafy
to comprehend why it could not be allowed in
the conftitution of a common Jury, fince it
would expofe them in the interval to all the
arts of feduction which might lie in wait for
them abroad, and which perfons of the ordinary rank might not always be able to refift.
Thefe cannot be fuppofed to operate upon the
perfons felected for this Tribunal, guarded as
they are againft all means of corruption or influence, by their rank, their ftation in life, and
above all, by that dignity and refponfibility of
character which is annexed to the fituation of
public men. When we add to this, the abfolute impoffibility of carrying through in one
day the detail of trials which do not turn, like

common

common cafes, upon the afcertainment of a fimple fact, but comprize various and complicated difcuffions, involving in them the choice of evils, and points of ftate neceffity, we muft confefs, that a power of adjournment is neceffary, for the firft purpofes of juftice; the hearing attentively, and at full length, the feveral allegations of the contending parties.

We are next to confider, how far it was expedient to difpenfe with the unanimity of their verdict. This feature is a ftriking peculiarity in the prefent conftitution of the Englifh Courts of Juftice : Whether it exifted in their original formation is uncertain : Indeed there is great reafon to think that it has crept in at a fubfequent period. It obtains in no other country, not even in Scotland, where Juries are cœval with their Government. In our higheft Court of Juftice, that of the Peers, it never has exifted ; nor has it been adopted in any tribunal which the wifdom of the Legiflature has found occafion to eftablifh ; not even in that moft nearly interefting to the Legiflature, which decides upon the legality of elections

tions to a feat in Parliament. The objections to it are fo forcible and fo obvious, from the poffibility, and indeed frequency, of thofe differences of opinion between honeft men, which feldom yield to mutual argument, that the moft celebrated writers on this fubject have queftioned its policy. Yet how infinitely are thefe objections increafed by the nature of the caufes to be heard before this Court. Perhaps in the ordinary courfe of civil caufes, where the fact is fimple, and open to the comprehenfion of every plain underftanding, there may be little reafon for apprehending fuch difference of opinion. But in caufes relative to India, at once complicated in their nature, and including in them confiderations of political and commercial intereft, fuch differences of opinion muft not only often happen, but may originate on both fides, in principles of ftrict duty, and in the dictates of a fcrupulous confcience.

The laft deviations from the forms of a Jury, is that which conftitutes them Judges of the Law, as well as the Fact: And againft this, particular clamour feems to have been

raifed,

raifed, though perhaps with far the leaft fhew
of reafon. For, *on the one hand*, it is a power
which our Conftitution allows and recognizes
in innumerable inftances, not only in Courts
Martial, but in all proceedings before Juftices
of the Peace; before Courts of Quarter
Seffions; in our Courts of Law, upon attach-
ments; and laftly, in the proceedings of Parliament, as well in cafes of impeachment, as in
that eftablifhed mode of trial, which every
Peer claims as his deareft birth-right—the pri-
vilege of being tried, in cafes affecting his life
or his honour, by the whole body of the
Peerage fitting in judgement upon him, and
deciding, as in the inflance of this Tribunal,
both the Fact and the Law, as well as pro-
nouncing fentence. And, *on the other hand*,
it may be queftioned, whether it is really any
deviation; and whether Juries are not competent to judge of the Law as well as the Fact.
For certainly, whenever Juries take upon themfelves, as in the cafe of *Almon*, and more re-
cently in that of Dean *Shipley*, to pronounce
the fact true, but the intention not illegal,
they do in reality exercife that very power
which is now to be vefted in this Tribunal.

But

But fuppofing it to be that innovation which
it has been vainly contended to be, ftill in the
prefent inftance it would be unavoidable. For,
fince in all cafes before this Court, the quan-
tum of punifhment muft depend upon the circumftances which induce them to find the de-
linquent guilty, there would be a manifeft de-
fect, if thofe who had confidered the one were
not alfo to determine the other. And fuppofing this power to be left to the three Judges,
it might then happen that a fentence might be
paffed, meafured only by their feperate opinion,
and very difproportionate to the fenfe which
the reft of the Court might have of his guilt :
And it would be in vain for the majority to
condemn, if three of the number could deftroy the effect of their verdict, by their lenity
in meafuring the punifhment.

In furveying this Tribunal, we have found
it affimilated in every effential circumftance, to
the fpirit and practice of the Englifh Law
and carrying with it every benefit which re
fults from that peculiar mode of trial, which
Englifhmen fo juftly regard with pride, and
watch with jealoufy; differing from it in thofe
                                                minute

minute *forms* alone, which have little weight or fignificance, beyond what cuftom and antiquity has given them. And this is a meafure which afforded the faireft plea to the Minifter, of widening the bafis of his power, completed in a manner which entirely excludes the interference of the Crown, and clofes up all the avenues of Minifterial Influence.

Much has been faid upon the fubject of the *evidence* which is to be received before this Court; as if this part of the Bill was not only an infringement of the practice of the Engliſh Law, but a direct violation of the eternal principles of Juftice itfelf. But thefe objections, like the others which have been raifed againft this Bill, are conceived in ignorance, or fuggefted in malice. It is faid, that by the provifions for tranfmitting to the Court of King's Bench examinations taken in India, before Engliſh Judges, under all the forms and regulations of Engliſh Law, and for permitting the authentic records of the Company to be produced before the new Tribunal, an *unknown fpecies of evidence* is to be introduced into this Country. If they were in truth an innovation,

it

it would be eafy to prove that it is of indifpenfable neceffity to every idea of a trial of
Indian Delinquencies. And here too we might
plead the confeffion of Mr. *Fox,* who in the
debate on this very Bill, affented to thefe claufes,
even before they were modified to that ftate
in which we now fee them. But our argument
will reft on more folid grounds than any
affertion of that gentleman, or than any reafoning of mere neceffity. Whoever will have
recourfe to our Statute Books in one inftance,
and to the Reports of the Court of King's
Bench in the other, will find that a Law was
already in exiftence for taking depofitions in
India, under a Commiffion from the King's
Bench; and that the Records of the Company
were actually read in evidence, under the authority of Lord Mansfield, in the Trial of Mr.
Stratton. What then fhall we fay of thofe
Legiflators, Members alfo of the higheft Court
of Juftice in this kingdom, who, in their zeal
againft the paffing of this Act, have repro-
bated as innovations, * things eftablifhed by
law, and fanctioned by practice; and *have re-
corded to pofterity, their total ignorance of the*

H                    *laws*

* Vide Lords' Proteft, Auguft 9, 1784.

*laws under which they are themselves protected,
and by which they are to judge of the properties
and lives of others.* But to fome of them,
*protefts* on this fubject are ominous. A few
incoherent words, half-uttered in broken fen-
tences, may be tortured into meaning, and
mifreprefented into fenfe. But thefe written
opinions remain, and rife in judgement againft
them, to prove, that while they affect to mo-
nopolize the abilities and virtue of this country,
they *poffefs neither the knowledge to judge with
wifdom, nor the integrity to act with confiftency.*

Connected with the fubject of *Evidence,* is the
regulation which compels all Servants of the
Company, within two months after their return
from India, to deliver into the Court of Ex-
chequer, inventories of their property of every
kind, which they may then be poffeffed of,
The feverity of this is objected to; and yet it
would be difficult to find any other teft of the
conduct of their feveral officers, or any other
check to the force of thofe temptations, from
which fo much evil has already proceeded, and
fo much more is ftill to be apprehended. What
motives can we fuppofe fo ftrong, as the fhame
of

of returning after a short absence with a large property, or the pride of bringing home a very moderate fortune after a long residence in that Country, to stifle that spirit of avarice and rapacity, which has so long prevailed; and to secure the natives from that rapine and oppression, under which they have so long unfortunately laboured.

For a series of years, we have been accustomed to see every public measure, as it passed, converted to the purposes of Ministerial Influence. Not a tax was levied, but it was employed by the *unprincipled Minister of the day,* as a means of strengthening his power: And perhaps he was less scrupulous what new burthens he laid upon the people, when he found it the most successful method of invading their liberties. And within this last year, we have been witnesses to the eagerness with which another Ministerial Leader seized this very measure, relative to the regulation of the East Indies, as an instrument for giving a death-blow to the Constitution; treating the supposition of effecting any reform otherwise, as absurd and impracticable. What then must be our feelings of

surprize

furprize and admiration, when we find in the prefent Bill, this great work effected, without the minuteft acceffion of Patronage to Government: When we fee a Court of Judicature erected, inacceffible to influence either from the Crown or the Company; and behold a vaft Continent fubjected to the controul of this kingdom, without producing the fmalleft ill effect upon the Britifh Conftitution? When we contemplate fuch a Bill, may we not juftly confider it as an *emblem* of the PURITY and INTEGRITY of the mind from whence it has proceeded; and may we not draw conclufion highly favourable to the intentions, and calculated to infpire confidence in the conduct of the prefent MINISTER of this Country.

MR.

www.ingramcontent.com/pod-product-compliance
Lightning Source LLC
Chambersburg PA
CBHW031809090426
42739CB00008B/1227